Heartbreak Heaux-Tales. Copyright © 2021 by Kay Price. All rights reserved. No part of this book may be used or reproduced in any manner whatsoever without written permission except in the case of brief quotations embodied in critical articles and reviews. For information, address The Write Away LLC, PO Box 61, Harvey, LA 70059.

ISBN: 978-1-7366779-1-9

Contents

Acknowledgment	6
Introduction	7
Narration 1	*10*
Mental Lovin	11
What I See	13
Bound by a Vow	14
Narration 2	*16*
In My Mind	17
Say Something	19
Blame Me	20
Never Ever	22
Narration 3	*23*
Questions That Need Answers	24
Narration 4	*25*
Chapter Closed	26
Heartbreak Romance	27
Narration 5	*29*
Spontaneity	30
Narration 6	*32*
Used	33

Narration 7	*35*
Never to be Understood	36
Contradictions	38
Realizations	40
Narration 8	*42*
The Man for Me	43
Narration 9	*45*
Just Sex	46
I Can't Forget You	49
Addiction	51
Narration 10	*53*
A Better Me	54
Narration 11	*56*
Pep Talk	57
Narration 12	*59*
Perfect…Total… Bliss	60
Inconsistency	63
Narration 13	*65*
King Switch Up	66
Twin Flame	68
Narration 14	*70*
Walk Away	71

Narration 15	*74*
N-A-S-T-Y	75
Narration 16	*77*
Ruthless	78
Narration 17	*80*
Reminiscing	81
If You Were Here Right Now	85
Sex Games	87
Narration 18	*89*
Broken Chains	90
The Truth	92
Narration 19	*94*
My Fault	95
Final Straw	96
Narration 20	*98*
The Bounceback	99
Giving In	101
Narration 21	*103*
Dear Narcissist	104
Afterword	107
Heaux Phase	108

Acknowledgment

First and foremost, I want to give a huge shout out to my therapist because homeboy was relentless when it came to pulling these emotions out. I definitely would not have done this without his encouragement. I'd also like to thank my very small circle of support for the listening ears, positive words, and proof reading. I had no idea what I was doing, but as I made progress ideas kept coming and I am proud of the final product.

Lastly, I have to give credit where credit is due and thank all of the people that played a role in getting me here. Recapping these experiences gave me a sense of self that I've never had. Talk about growth! Life is good.

Introduction

It was always easier for me to say things than it was for me to write. I kept my hands restrained in a stupid attempt to fight. Because everytime I'd write, tears would fill the page. And I'd release emotions I had locked into this cage...

I've finally gained the courage to free myself. This book tells the story of everything I've felt and some of the things I've been through since "being out in the real world." I'm no longer embarrassed about it. This started as a therapy project, but turned into an opportunity for me to really let go; to move on. Hopefully, it encourages others to do the same. I read a quote throughout this process by Paulo Coelho that said *"Tears are words that need to be written"* and…well… I present to you my tears.

Heartbreak Heaux-Tales
(A book of poems to tell my story)

So it started with this guy. I was so caught up in him that I wanted to make love to more than his body; I felt I needed to fuck his mind....

"Mental Lovin"

I want to make love to you
But not just sexually
I want to get so deep
As to make you climax intellectually

I want you to trust me
Because I'll need you opened up
I want a connection
Something more than a good fuck

There's nothing wrong with love making
I know I can satisfy you intimately
But come on, be real
How many females have made you come mentally

I want to relax your body
As well as your mind
After my mental loving
You'll be temporarily blind

Now I am being a little arrogant
And that I can admit
But if we can connect mentally
It's better than just sensations of penises and clits

It's so much better than just a nut
Because it goes well beyond the physical
I can take you to new heights
And give you pleasure deeper than the spiritual

Just give me a try
I promise I'm not teasing you
I'll have you begging for this loving
Because I'm that confident in pleasing you

I can give you an orgasm
Without the fondling, kissing, or cuddling
Just let me know you want some more
And I'll bless you with this mental loving

"What I See"

They say what is it in you I see...
I see the man for me.
I see a man with compassion and drive.
With something to lose and nothing to hide.
I see a man with ambition and pride
Who can express his feelings inside.
I see a man who lives hopefully,
Optimistic and openly.
Hard-working and caring
Who has no problem sharing.
I see a man offering the little he has
While asking for nothing in return.
A man who wants only my time
But also makes my skin burn.
I see a man who makes me happy
Who's responsible for my smile
A man that can admit he's in LOVE
Without being in denial.
I see a man who understands
What it means to be a man.
I see a man who's not afraid
To bow before his woman.
Because he recognizes me as royalty
And he can handle the needs of his Queen.
I see a man who gives me loyalty
Who's fit to be MY KING!
You may never see in him what I see
Because I'm convinced THIS man was built
exclusively for me...

"Bound By A Vow"

I was chasing something in someone
that you brought to me so freely.
Who knew love could be this easy,
so emotionally healing?
You make this effortless,
I still can't explain the feeling...

I doubted true love for so long,
I thought it was unreal.
But there's nothing else to explain
the crazy way I feel.
Every moment with you
is perfect yet and still...

I remember questioning
do soulmates really exist?
But that thought quickly left my mind
the moment that we kissed.
And my past became irrelevant
just something to dismiss...

I started to bloom so beautifully,
thorns disappearing from this rose.
My heart began to melt
and it was like it never froze.
You bring out the best in me
as our love continuously grows...

So here I stand before you
with a vow thats far too short,
dedicating myself to you;
From here is where WE start!
A family in the making
that won't be torn apart.
A vow that I can make because I feel it in my
heart...

And shortly after that… he was gone. My emotions were all over the place and naturally, my mind followed.

"In My Mind"

A little seed planted
Giant ideas grow
Things taken for granted
But you never really know
Many words spoken
But actions aren't taken
Now I'm disappointed
And a little bit impatient

Promises broken
Emotions running high
As reality sets in
The tears drop from my eye
Sitting in silence
Buried deep in thought
Trying to ignore the pain
That's building in my heart.

Muffling my cries
An idea in my brain
That you lied about EVERYTHING
Cuz you had something to gain.
So how do I address this
Without being mean?
Was it all just a lie?
Was I really being green?

I dedicated myself
To you and ONLY you
Did I fall in love with someone
Who was never being true?
A means to an end...
Is that what I was?
Do you love me any
Or did you say that just because?

A little seed planted
Love started to grow
Was it ever really real?
I guess I'll never know
Expressing myself fully
I made it pretty clear
I opened up to you
Said I'd always be here
But you don't even care
I was never your attraction
You gave up the girl that would give you the world
Because you weren't ready to take action.

"SAY SOMETHING"

I'M PISSED
I'M TIRED OF YOUR SHIT
I WILL NOT BE DISMISSED
THIS TIME I MUST PERSIST
THAT YOU SAY SOMETHING...

I'M TIRED
I NEED TO HEAR YOUR SIDE
DON'T TELL ME NO MORE LIES
DON'T SIT THERE AND BE QUIET
SAY SOMETHING!

I'M COOL
I WILL NOT PLAY THE FOOL
WAITING FOR THE TRUTH
THIS TIME I'M REALLY THROUGH
IF YOU DON'T SAY SOMETHING!

"BLAME ME"

I wanted something better for you than you wanted for yourself
I didn't realize before that's why you denied my help
Wasting energy trying to build you up while you tore yourself down
And after draining all my energy you decide not to stick around?
You got to pack up your things and leave without saying a word
I fussed soooo much because I was always going unheard
But you want to play the victim like the character you are
Just a weak man with insecurities that won't get you very far
You called me abusive because I shot down all your lies
And the truth is you provoked me into wounding all your pride
Trying to keep things from me, but couldn't play both sides
Ya girl's a PI, and you're trying to live two lives?
You were acting like the child you said I treated you as

I gave you every chance to be a man, but instead you crashed.
So yes, I pointed out your errors and all the stupid decisions
Cuz I was pushing for greatness and trying to move with precision
Fighting a battle that I thought we could win as a team
But you were fighting against me, so I started to scream
And you can say it's all my fault, cool I'll take all the blame...
For believing in a man with nothing to his name
For loving too hard while being too outspoken
For thinking you were strong and not easily broken
For pushing you too hard because you were scared to fail
For not realizing sooner that your ego had been frail
For missing all the signs that said your mind was weak
For being too damn strong for a man so damn meek!

"Never Ever"

I loved you enough to marry you-
Something I said I'd never do.
I even thought about having your kid-
Glad that's something I never did.
I never ever thought you would walk away
I never ever thought that you wouldn't stay
And then the way you did it was bitch ass
I never thought that you could make me this sad!

I cried my eyes out for a whole week
Always had words, but couldn't speak
Ignored every phone call and missed text
I never ever dealt with such neglect
Slept my days away, wouldn't wake up
This is some shit I can't make up
I stalked your FB, thought you had to die
Could've killed you 10 times- I was justified

I never ever thought I could hurt so bad
I never ever thought I could be so mad
Almost packed a suitcase and caught a flight
Just to show you what my hurt felt like
A bunch of crazy shit I thought I would do
I knew there was nothing to convince you
I gave you my best- I loved you like a clown
Wish I had NEVER EVER let my guard down…

And even with all the anger and regret, I still had questions.

"Questions That Need Answers"

Can we fix what was broken?
Can we stop what's in motion?
Or did I hurt you too much?
Did I leave your heart crushed?

Are you mad or don't care?
Have we lost what was there?
Was I harsh, was I mean?
Is there more to be seen?

Do you still feel the pain?
Does it hurt all the same?
Do you ever stop and wonder?
Do you think we can recover?

Did I push you away?
Did we need the delay?
Do I still fuel your hunger?
Can we be even stronger?

Do I still give you chills?
Are you still in your feels?
Can the love be revived
If I just apologize?

Deep inside I already knew the answers. I had to take things for what they were and move on. So… that's what I did.

"Chapter Closed"

Everything happens for a reason

It's a blessing or a lesson

But that doesn't stop the pain

Or the anger and aggression

And I know it will get better

Yes, I know that I'll be good

But it hurts like I'm cursed

I know you did the best you could

You tried to make me happy

If only just a smile

So I appreciate the effort

Though you only stayed a while

"Heartbreak Romance"

I broke a promise to you and gave away something that was yours
I couldn't fight the feeling with lust oozing through my pores
I never planned on actually doing it, but I wanted to feel good
And he broke through every barrier like I only thought you could

Every memory got erased for that very short while
As my feeling of neglect got released on a towel
And my pent up frustrations all came pouring out
As I relaxed completely ignoring all the roaring doubt

I was taken on a ride so wild that I completely lost myself
I got so high and lost control like I was someone else
Kind of like a child, rebelling and acting out for a thrill
Just a little something to overpower all the pain I feel

What I never expected was for his passion to be so great
Or for him to take over my body and completely dominate
For him to prove how much he wanted me if only for a night
For him to cloud my judgment and make everything seem right

I know that it was wrong, but I needed to release
I just wanted to feel good, but he swept me off my feet
I thought that I could do it without getting attached
But the joke's on me because I think I may have met my match

I pulled away he pulled me back and wrapped me in his arms
I felt safe in his space; the shelter from my storms
But when my high came down, all those feelings returned
And it was a never ending lesson that I was refusing to learn…

Because… well…
we kept fucking (shrugs)

"Spontaneity"

It didn't matter where we did it

In the bedroom, in the kitchen

In the shower, on the counters

The whole place was ours

So we fucked on all the floors

Got pinned up on all the doors

Even did it in the car

And that's how he got that scar

We did it on every chair

Did it through our underwear

He would do me on the dryer

The vibrations took me higher

So we tried it on the washer

The spin cycle made it harsher

We would fuck just too damn much

Did it anywhere we touched

We always enjoyed each other

Left white spots on all the covers

I think I came on every bed

On the headboard he got head

And we fucked and fucked and fucked

He sucked, I sucked, we sucked

He pleased me on the couch

My orgasms shook the house

We even tried it on the table

But we really weren't able

So we did it on the sink

And we didn't even think

There were times we had to rush

We were so spontaneous

At this point, sex was really all I wanted. It made me feel better, but I began to realize I didn't even like this dude. Like, not even a little.

"Used"

I never really even liked him

But our sex was good

We were trying to bust nuts

And that was understood

There were many late nights

Even more orgasms

His dick was legit

Always made the pussy spasm

I would cum and before I could come down, I was

cumming again

We would make it a game

And he would always win

His head hit different

He must've wrote the book

He put his mouth on me and my whole world shook

But I never really liked him

He just made me forget

He gave me dick on demand

I didn't have to commit

So we kept messing around

He would ask me to stay

I could tell that he was mad

Every night I slipped away

And we'd argue then fuck

Because he fucked me the best

As long as I was busting nuts

I wasn't worried about the rest

I was over catching feelings

I couldn't handle being hurt

And despite my opposition

He'd still fill me with girth...

But I never really liked him

I played this game for a few months before I allowed my thoughts to drift back to that damn ex-husband. I wanted to understand things I never would. I had more questions. But after weeks of reflecting, I took a step back and concluded, "Damn. Maybe I was a lil difficult."

"Never to be Understood"

I don't understand how you cannot understand
Or why you thought me joking when I'd say you're my man
Or why you'd think I was running game and playing around
When I was only being honest about the love I thought I found.

I don't understand how you can't understand
Opening up to you showed that feelings had changed
I thought you were different, I thought that you'd care
But you made it clear you didn't, like I never was there

Its like we never had anything and there was never any love
As if we didn't complement each other like a hand & a glove
And it hurts so bad that you could just turn away
How could you leave me like that when I begged you to stay?

I don't understand how you cannot understand
That giving you LOVE did not come with a plan
I wasn't plotting and scheming or using the word lightly
I was giving you a title that I thought you deserved rightly

And yet I don't understand how you can't understand
That I was giving my heart and all I got was the blame
I tried to show you that I would have traded my soul
You must have thought me a lie because you acted so cold

But I don't understand how you could doubt me so much
That you'd play the shit out me like you did in a rush
When did you stop believing in me without reason?
It was supposed to be forever, never just for a season

I just don't understand how you don't understand
Or how you make my concerns seem like such a demand
And how you can just tell me that I shouldn't trip
When you let me give myself to you knowing you'd dip

But I did what you said and I stopped trippin
Promised myself I'd never again get caught slippin
Don't expect me to react when I've already given up
Don't come asking for me back once I no longer give a fuck!

"CONTRADICTIONS"

Why do we create our own problems
And play dangerous, unfair games
Why do we aim to deceive each other
When we're really just the same

Why do we mess around with fire
Then complain of getting burned
Why do we try to teach lessons
About thing we have never learned

Why do we agree to monogamy
And still go out and mess around
Why look for things in other people
That we have already found

Why do we only chase the highs
And cower from the lows
Caught up in karma and mad
Because we're reaping what we sow

Why do we try to save things
That shouldn't really be saved
Why do we try and take things
That we never even gave

It never made sense, but still
We do it over and over
The irony of life
And we don't realize until we're older

We're walking contradictions
Every. Single. Day
Saying we want things
But acting differently

"REALIZATIONS"

I think I finally get it
It's starting to make sense
You were only being a man
Responding to my unhappiness
I was stressing and lashing out
I didn't know how to cope
And you were dealing with your own demons
So I started to lose hope
I wasn't getting the support I needed
So I stayed in my masculine phase
Searching for solutions to your problems
Instead of nurturing my female ways
I couldn't stop the love I had for you
I just needed time for talking
But every time I made it home
I walked into you sulking
And I just wanted to share my day
But instead I pulled away
Because I needed your full attention
For you to listen to what I'd say
You were distracted often, I know
You just couldn't move on
From all your bad decisions
And I could no longer be strong
I felt overwhelmed and defeated
And together we grew weaker
I became more hopeless every day
Watching you sink deeper
You needed me to pull you out
But you wasn't a swimmer
The light that shined so bright before
Continued to get dimmer

I never wanted to be the strongest
I only wanted to help you lead me
I became insensitive to your sensitivity
And how much you could need me
So this was never all your fault
And you should never feel that way
You tried to make me happy
But I stripped it all away

Now at this point, I thought I had things figured out. I thought I knew what I needed in my next man, so I was like, "Let's manifest this shit real quick."

"The Man For Me"

I need a man who can admit defeat
And let me help him when he's down
I need a man who can accept a queen
One not afraid to embrace his crown

I need a man who can communicate
Someone who listens when I speak
But who will not avoid confrontation
A man that can stand up to me

I need a man that can adapt to change
A man who can give me a plan
Who will work with me and accept me
As we strive to raise our clan

I need a man that can take charge
But who can also accept advice
Especially when his plans don't work
And things aren't going quite right

I need a man that can express himself
A man who's honest and sincere
He won't cower to my temper
And he'll always be here...

I need a man whose ego is big
Whose confidence is loud
One who dominates the room
And stands out in a crowd

I need a man who can hold his own
And put the dick down
A man to put me in my place
Without even a sound

So while I waited for my manifestation to surface, I went back to what I knew. And when we weren't actually doing things, I thought about all the other things I did. I needed to stay distracted. The shit was crazy!

"Just Sex"

Let's have nice slow, lick me low, from head to toe sex
With ass smackin, back scratchin, breath catchin next
I want mind blowin, juices flowin, orgasms growin
With my head in the chair, ass in the air, and your hands in my hair
I want it to be so good that my legs lock and my heart stops,
Goin into convulsing shocks as my eyes pop...

I'm talkin jaw droppin, bed rockin, headboard knockin sex
Demanding what to do next, but you know all about that!
You crack a grin ask where I've been and say, "Girl don't tease me!"
But I'm not a tease, this is what I need, so I respond, "Can you please me?"
And you take your time, but I don't mind as you kiss me from behind

With my neck cocked and our eyes locked, my panties drop
In disbelief that I went there, but in this game anything's fair...
You take some time to stop and stare, too bad you have to share
You know I've always desired you, so let us do what we do.
And baby, it is time to please so drop down to your knees.
I spread my legs, and pull your dreads as your tongue goes in with ease.

My hips buck, your face is fucked, and my ass cheeks are squeezed.
Then they're slapped, you make them clap, and I'm suddenly relieved.
You catch me as we hit the floor, we've done this times before
You try to stand, but I demand we won't do this no more.
Surprisingly, you agree... and I knew it wasn't me
So I give you a look, I see you're shook, tell me, "who is she?"

But you won't talk no more, so I come and back it up?
And you gon snatch it up, I wanna feel you smack this up.
Let me throw it back, but don't give it back, just keep it.
The best fuck of both our lives; one of our biggest secrets.
Then when we're done with our fun, you can go and treat your girl
And hopefully my man won't come and try to eat the pearl
Because we giving it to each other and tonight will be our last
Remember all this nastiness when you're out there living fast
Saying, "It's just sex. It's just sex," but you keep on coming back
You know there's no one else out there that's fucking you like that

"I Can't Forget You"

I still think about you...
Even with my man's head buried between my thighs, I'm
still feigning for you.
Your essence gave me a high.
Never smoked a day in my life, but I stayed choked up as
we made love and I looked into your eyes.

I can still smell you...
Your scent sticks in my nostrils like too much bleach in a
room with a closed door.
I can taste you like I ate you a million times before.

I can still see you...
Solid, statuesque, confident in your nakedness.
I can feel the flames start to consume me as my mind
travels down a path of destruction and
recklessness.

I swear I still feel you...
Like an electric shock to my soul.
When bae is deep inside me and I start to lose control.
Eyes closed, lips parted; we should have finished what we
started but I let my hand fold.

Then soon I folded too.
My words grew; loud, proud and obnoxious
And I lost you. Now you're just a picture in my pocket.
But I remember the way I loved you.

Needing you, but denying the way I felt inside.
Can you even believe that shit still eats me alive?
I will never forget you...
And you'll never know how much I tried

"Addiction"

The room stays dark and cold
Indian style with my eyes closed
Silence fills da air
But I can hear you everywhere

Skin tingling, sweat dripping
Body's hot, mind tripping
Sitting, rocking back and forth
The balls no longer in my court

Shaking, scratching, sniffling
My head's ringing, body stiffens
Mouth parched, eyes bucked
Curled up with my head tucked

Blank stare, clearly dazed
Stuck up in this stupid phase
Wanting, fiening, needing it
With nothing here worth feeding it

Nothing here to feed the high
Nothing to block the burn inside
So I jump up in a haste
My heart races, my feet pace

I'm falling, drowning, crashing
No energy left as the days keep passing
So the dope man asks what I need
X, coke, shrooms, or speed?

And I scratch my head as if to think
Hospital, rehab, meds, or shrink?
I hit the floor as my chest tightens
Muscle spasms and I can't fight it

I know that none of his drugs will do
Because my choice of drug was always you...

Eventually, everything became too much. "We" became too much. The thoughts became too much. The pressure became too much. But I felt that I had matured pass what was taking place in those moments. So I dipped out again. This time, for good.

"A Better Me"

I am strong, I have grown

I know what I can take

You push my limits constantly

But I will never break

Still a work in progress

But I've come oh so far

I stuck in there and cared

While you showed me who you are

Selfish, confused, and insecure

You thought I'd stick around

And keep on putting up with you

As you tried to bring me down

I kept being forgiving

Dismissing what I knew

Thinking you were ahead

While I was playing the fool

Dealing with your attitude

Tolerating your lies

Ignoring negative behaviors

Giving you more tries

Showing I could tolerate you

Even at your meanest

That I could still be kind

I had to be the GREENEST!

I told you you'd be nice eventually

But it took you too long

"You'll miss the way I cared for you

When I'm already gone"

You were just a lesson

So let's make no mistake

I put up with the bullshit

To prove my patience great

You made a better me

Now I knew from the start where this next chapter was going, but…. Shit happened. And it happened fast!

"Pep Talk"

Don't get attached

Repeat it, repeat it, repeat it

You're involved with a narcissist

And I need you to see it.

The more people know it

The harder it is to hide

Those emotions, don't you show it

Better push them shits aside

He says one thing

While doing the opposite

Reiterating his lies

Feeding you bullshit

But don't you fall for it

You know how this goes

Making you think you're happy

Straight gas-lighting you hoes

But you can see right through it

Although you don't believe it

You tolerate the foolery

Like how did he conceive this?

You think you can be content

But is it really true?

Have you let this little devil

Out manipulate you?

You've played this game before

You have never lost

So let's not start right now

You shall win at any cost...

Now whether I really won or not is debatable, but things were good… until they weren't.

"Perfect...Total...Bliss"

You want another night of ecstasy?
Perfect...total...bliss?
Panting and awaiting anxiously
For that simple little kiss
The one that will spark the fire
And set us both ablaze
Then lead to the exciting stuff
That will set us in a daze
An erotic "Ahhhhh"...
Followed by my name
Along with a moan so strong
It makes me go insane
So I take you down slowly
And pretend to let you guide me
But I love it when you say,
"You know what to do to satisfy me!"
And I'll do anything you want
All you have to do is ask

Because my sole goal
Is to make you reach climax
Talk about excitement
Nothing turns me on more
Than my getting your rocks off
And you leaving my ass sore
So I take pride in this
I'm a master at this 'game'
And I know I'm playing it right
Because I heat you like a flame
Talking to you dirty
The blood pulsates through our veins
You grab my hair and smack my ass
As you beat it out the frame
We always agree, "This the last time"
But I know it's never the last
Because we're at our best together
I love giving you this ass
Now I know I can talk shit
But you know I can relieve you
And no one does it better

I'm the best one to please you

I'm your drug

You're addicted to me

This is PERFECT...TOTAL BLISS

So I guess we're meant to be...

"Inconsistency"

I want to be wrapped around you
Bodies close together and warm
Leg thrown over yours as I wrap you in my arms.

Snuggled, breathing in your scent
Caressing the hairs on your chest
Pushing my pelvis into you while kissing down your neck.

I used to feel so safe like this
I craved for your touch
It wasn't long before I knew you didn't deserve my trust.

But yet and still, I loved you
And all the potential you showed
Consistently inconsistent then the admiration slowed.

I doubted many things
But my feelings, I felt sure
Every time we kissed I knew the love was raw and pure

But I couldn't get too close
Because deep down I knew
That she was still a factor and yall had something too.

So I often "brushed you off"
I didn't want to make you choose
Before it was all said and done I already knew you'd lose

I knew your inconsistency would push us both away
We wanted black or white,
But you kept things painted gray

Consistently inconsistent
Different, every time you came
Soon I made a choice and then I became the same.

Unmatched words and actions
Walking contradictions
Lying to ourselves living life in two dimensions

Ignoring all the signs
Fighting what was felt
Rolling with the punches, playing the cards that we were dealt

Consistently inconsistent
Now we're pass the point of help
Keeping up a game but ended up playing yourself...

I became something I wasn't. I was so angry. I think I was actually just mad at myself for being a reflection of everything I despised. But there was something about this dude that forced me to project his actions. He was……

"King Switch Up"

Smooth with the lines
Know just what to say
He can reel them in
Then, throw them away
He just wants a friend
And he likes to date
Loves being a bachelor
But wants a mate
He can sleep around
He can be exclusive
So he does them both
He's just so illusive
And he doesn't know
Why shit never works
He be switching up
Leaving females hurt...

So they fall out
Then he slides back in
Straight into fucking
But "she's just a friend"

Kissing foreheads
Stealing souls
And the next day
He's acting cold
Won't do you right
But won't let you quit
Will fuck you raw
But won't commit
Getting hopes high
Then flipping shit up
Tread with caution
He's King Switch Up

"Twin Flame"

Mirroring each other
It's like we share a brain
Scarred by our past hurts and all we know is pain
So that is what we cause
And then we pass the blame
Caught up in a circus, dancing with my twin flame

Late night conversations
Kept me in my head
I always wondered how I let him get me in his bed
I used to buy his stories
Believed everything he said
Despite my doubts I took a walk on all the bricks he laid

Crazy I can think back
Remember all the feels
The way that he would touch me and leave me with the chills
How I shut down from him
Feeling things unreal
How he could lie and lie again and I could love him still?

Hurting, but holding on
Because I believed in this
I knew the moment we laid down that things would be intense
And we said we didn't want that
But we kept taking the risk
I never stopped to shoot my shot cuz I was scared to miss

Toying with other people
We could have had a home
Building up a house of bricks instead of casting stone
But we wouldn't be together
And didn't want to be alone
Being immature instead of being grown

And I finally made the choice I should had been made...

"Walk Away"

I walked into this situation with only one expectation
But here I am now disappointed
I was tolerating shit that I would never deal with
Just to get what I wanted
And he failed me.
All I asked for was honesty,
But consistently he lied to me
And ironically, karma handled the rest.
But I didn't know of the forces already in motion,
So I escalated the mess.
I mean the only job a mirror has is to reflect,
So I reflected.
And every time I was neglected,
I rejected him.
But he just couldn't lose
And he wouldn't choose
Because he wanted us both.
I kept trying to break free and let go,
But he kept anchoring the boat.

Now this is what we've become;
Two scorned individuals playing a game
Both with the aim of keeping the score tied.
But it could have all been avoided if he hadn't lied.
And he just can't accept his part in this
Because he won't admit his heart's in this
And neither will I.
So we talk but we don't hear each other.
Nagging him like I'm his mother
Cuz he wants me to act like he's my brother
But we still fuckin though.
This nigga is literally a fucking joke.
And, now I know...

I am no longer at peace.
Having a clear frame of mind is more important to me than having a release.
Therefore, I know that this relationship must cease.
I cannot keep allowing myself to fall victim to his whit because if I do then he'll never quit.
And I need this to be over before my heart grows any colder.
The weight of my hate breaks my shoulders
And crushes me just the same.
The feeling is relentless and though I'm filled with resentment,
I'm hopeful that he will change.

But it will never be the same
And all of the pain reminds me
That my hopefulness is senseless.
He will always be a hindrance to my happiness.
And I just can't let that happen
So I must walk away.
There's no more words that I can say
That will make things different
Next time I'll listen
Before I get this way.

After months of suppressing feelings, desires, and needs, I relapsed... H-A-R-D!

"Nasty"

I didn't come to play this time
Forget the good girl act
I'm trying to fuck out my frustrations
I'm trying to throw this back
No cuddles my nigga
I want you to hold me down
I need you to punish this pussy
Like I had messed around

I'm not here for the small talk
I want to get choked up
No snuggles or kisses either
I'm just here to be stroked up
So don't you take your time
I need this nut quickly
Make this pussy sneeze
Like, "Goddamnit, is she sickly?"

I want you to take control of me
Put me on my knees
Force my chest on the bed
And make me beg you please
Bite me on my shoulders
As you roughly hold my hips
Beat this pussy senseless
My love handles are your grips

Wrap your fingers in my hair
I want my ass smacked
Fuck me like you're pissed
And make this pussy talk back
Make my words run together
Only moans leave my mouth
Go long, go deep, go harder
Until my cum is spilling out

But don't you show me mercy
Push me to my brink
Fuck my ass unconscious
Til I can no longer think
Fucking out my frustrations
Coming across trashy
But I don't really care no more
I just want to be NASTY!

But it didn't stop the pain this time… So, I reverted back to very old toxic behavior. Behavior I had worked very hard to leave behind.

"Ruthless"

Every time I think back to what got me here, it hurts all over again.
And for that, with me, you will never win.
I don't want to be around you, I don't want you as a friend.
This baby here between us is all that keeps me in...
The only reason I'm cordial and answer when you call.
The reason I'm not at your place and burning down your walls.
We could have had it all, but instead you wanted games, so I showed you how to ball.
Hurt people hurt people, that's how the story goes
But I'm the worst type of hurt because it never shows
And no one ever really knows...
What I'm capable of once my rage grows

I warned you! I told you, "be careful with me..."
So now I must show you how careless I can be
Delete your shit, become a bitch, then up and disappear
Have you standing around like, "how did I get here"
So confused by my muse thinking you couldn't lose
That you actually convinced yourself you were being used
Flipping shit around, but you played us all the same
Thinking you could really win at my favorite game...
But I'm ruthless!

And when I became this way, everything became SEX! But since I wouldn't allow anyone else to have access to me in that way, I allowed my thoughts to linger on past experiences.

"Reminiscing"

I'm reminiscent
Thinking about the way you fucked me
No love or sympathy, no nothing
But the way you sucked me.... (whew)
You had me believing it was something
If only in that moment when you would grope me
And when you stroked me...
Precise, persistent, consistent
Until I no longer resisted
Boy you were relentless
Clearly, I kinda miss it... (Right)
The only nigga who could call me and I'd slip out in the night.
I mean, you did EVERYTHING I liked.
Moaning in my ear telling me how my pussy tight.
Slapping my ass and gripping my hips, demanding I throw it back.
And before I know it, I can't control it, the bed is soaking wet.

Legs shaking... they ALWAYS shook
I remember the first time,
I wanted to rewind because of how you made me look.
Had me panting and flinching as you opened me up.
Trying to get me to relax as you filled my cup.
The more you poked, the more I choked
Back those moans dancing in my throat.
But I couldn't hold back the puddle that formed
As you paused just long enough to wrap me in your arms
And force the rest of you through.
I tensed like a virgin and it was then I knew
That I should probably stay the hell away from you.
BUT... here I am reminiscing.
And this is the first time in a long time
That I've thought, "Just one more time"
How I want to come on your dick just one more time.
How I want you to stroke my clit just one more time.

And give my pussy a lick just one more time.
Then hopefully, I can clear my mind.
Then I can focus.
Then I can stop spending my free time hoping,
Feeling hopeful that I could get that high again with someone else.
I've tried it.
And I know I denied it before,
But I've actually thought about just showing up at your door like,
"JUST ONE MORE TIME"
That feeling... you could never know that feeling I felt.
Every time you entered me, I'd melt.
I didn't even recognize myself
As I mumbled gibberish and you held me, pinned beneath you.
Digging deeper and deeper, but so slow
Until I felt that I could not take more.
Then you gave me more and BOOM!
I popped like a water balloon,
Gripping the sheets,
Biting your shoulder and gritting my teeth.
How many times could I hit my peak?

How many times could I not speak?
I underestimated your soul-snatching abilities.
You were killing me then bringing me back to life.
And I came on demand every time, so you never had to ask twice.
Now I lay here and think,
So caught up in thought that I don't blink
And then I notice my pussy is thumping.
My walls are crumbling and this feeling is so humbling
Because I had the pleasure of having you.
And boy, was it pleasurable,
But you'll never have me again.
Had me going all in
Every time you went all in
Now you cant even be my friend.
All you'll ever be is this story.
The guy that gave me all this Glory.

"If You Were Here Right Now"

I'd talk to you seductively and caress you slowly

Then lick you from head to toe holy

I'd touch your body and play with you solely

And afterwards I'd let you fold me

I'd relax you, giving you a massage

Then climb on top of you and give you a ride

Riding up and down slow then increasing my pace

Deliberate in my grind, watching the pleasure on your face

I'd make you cum hard then climb off

Leaving you confused between lust and love

As we catch our breaths before starting again

With you on top and ready to go in

Exhaling as you find your way into my walls

I'd pull you closer, wanting it all

As I wrap my hands around your neck

In sync with my legs wrapped around your back

Pulling you deeper between by thighs

Licking my lips, lids half closed, rolling my eyes

You'd start off fast and end up slow

And once I cum you'd lick me low

I'd give you pleasure as you give me mine

What's sex without exploring sixty-nine?

You'd reach your climax and explode in my mouth

I'd take it all in before spitting it all out

Flicking my tongue from shaft to base

I'm trying to take you to your special place

Making you want more, I stroke your dick to a tempo

Teasing you because I can't stay, I must go

But you know that if you were here right now

It's for sure that it would go down!

"Sex Games"

Every time I get horny, my first thought goes to you.
I hate myself for it, but it's the truth.
And I touch myself, thinking of how you touched me.
How good it felt when you fucked me.
The nights we'd lay in bed hugged up naked.
My bare ass against your hard dick, my back against your chest.
Your embrace around my waist as you brush against my breasts.
The way your hands glided down my side and landed between my thighs.
As your fingers parted my lips and your hips dip just enough to slide your dick inside.
Squeezing my cheeks and parting them.
Slow thrusting around my holes with your slick pole because your precum flows so easily.
I remember every way you enjoyed teasing me.
Kissing me gently then intensely.
Wrapping your fingers in my hair to tilt my head back so you could access my neck.
The feeling of security you gave me as you slaved me at the same time.
Coercing me to let you in while claiming it was all mine.
And I knew you were lying, but I wanted it.
I wanted to cum on your dick while letting you know it.
Every emotion I fought to hold back, you made me show it.
And I surrendered to you never realizing I was hindered by you.
Maybe I wanted to be anchored.

How could I be so blind, confiding in you?
Meanwhile you were lying to her and lying to me too.
...But I wanted it.
I wanted your body entwined with mine.
I wanted your lips on my lips sending chills down my spine.
I wanted my ass smacked while you hit it from behind.
Telling me to put my shoulders on the bed, nasty sloppy head while playing between my legs.
Telling me to let you know when I was cumming, knowing that's how I liked to cum.
Coming home every night for me to give you some.
And just doing this all again.
Every night for many nights, bodies wrapped together.
Even though I had better, it became a habit.
Like something I was fixed on and just had to have it.
And I guess she felt the same.
Both of us, just holding on, while you kept up the game.

This period of abstinence was my way to take back some control. It started to bring me clarity and hope.

"BROKEN CHAINS"

I know I will overcome this
But that doesn't stop the pain
I was trapped in a link of lies
And I couldnt break the chain
Despite my better judgement
I wanted what I wanted
And all those bad decisions
Will always keep me haunted
I wish I could take it back
I knew he was no good
Just a selfish little bastard
Taking advantage where he could
We know hurt people hurt people
But my faith was always strong
So I fought to get things right
When I knew they were all wrong
And I should've known better
But I thought we could be great
This was the closest I had come
And it ended in heartbreak
Making sacrifices for people
Who backed me into a wall
Leaving me to question
Why'd I ever risk the fall
And that was the biggest mistake
Here, look what this has got me
I'm right back at square one
But I'll never let it stop me

From being where I would've been
Had we never gotten involved
Had I never been convinced
That our problems would resolve
Had I never trusted him
Had we never had a child
Had I never accepted less
Than I ever would allow
Had I never lost myself
Had I just cut my ties
And allowed myself to feel
The pain I held inside
But I didn't, now I hate him
But I bet he'll still deny
That he purposely provoked me
With his secrets and his lies
Had I never given in
Had I never played his game
Had I just walked away
Before I became the blame
Had I never seeked revenge
Had I just stepped aside
Had I given myself permission to cry and
accepted our demise...
But I chose to keep trying
And then it was too late
I should've given up sooner,
Before he took all he could take
Now I'm stuck with resentment
I was so caught up with games
That I ended up hating him
As a way to break the chains

"THE TRUTH"

All you had to do was keep picking me

Don't be mad when another nigga's dicking me

I passed you the ball and you dropped it

Gave you all the GO'S and you stopped it

So don't come trying to convince me

That you always loved me and you miss me...

And you got your lil chicks in my inbox

Man just go on 'head and kick rocks

I heard all the shit that she been through

All the craziness dealing with you

All the stupid shit you been lying bout

Confirming everything I was calling out

And we can keep it moving right pass that

Stop trying to gas me up like I'm HAZMAT

Acting like you try to be a better man

But still ain't man enough to understand

All you had to do was apologize

For lying and trying to live double lives

Take accountability for our outcome

You were not the victim so don't play dumb

Stop telling people everyone's against you

Kept you in the game, but should've benched you

I was rooting hard, and look what I got

You chose people who treat yo ass like gym socks!

Eventually, I acknowledged that I was at fault for allowing a lot of the bullshit in this previous "situationship."

"My Fault"

I LET HIM LEAD THE STORIES
I LET HIM TELL HIS LIES
I LET HIM LIVE OUTSIDE THE BOX
WHILE KEEPING ME INSIDE

I LET HIM HAVE HIS WAY
I LET HIM DO HIS THING
I LET HIM WALK ALL OVER ME
WITHOUT HAVING A RING

I LET HIM LOVE ME WRONG
I LET HIM LIVE HIS LIFE
I LET HIM BE A HOE
WHILE I LIVED LIKE A WIFE

I LET HIM DRIVE ME CRAZY
I LET HIM MAKE ME SICK
I LET HIM MAKE HIS CHOICES
WHILE THINKING I'D BE PICKED

BUT I WAS NEVER WHAT HE WANTED
HE LOVED THE WAY I THOUGHT
HE LOVED WHAT I COULD DO FOR HIM
WITHOUT GIVING HIS HEART

"FINAL STRAW"

Don't think I didn't notice all the passive shit you did.

How you switched up too and how you dissed my kid.

I noticed all the petty actions and every step you took.

Childish behaviors; classic passive aggression textbook.

Your cowardly doings and fake memory lapses.

Acting like you don't react but I caught your reactions.

Wanting to seem unfazed, but I knew you were jealous

The quiet little storm; seeming sweet, baring malice.

So it wasn't unexpected that you'd want me neglected

Wanting me to hurt, but I was still unaffected

Didn't have the heart to say you ain't want me to stay

You knew your passive aggression would push me away

It's crazy how the "realest" ones are actually so fake

But I was fooled into thinking things were so great

And out of all my failed "relationships", this one took the cake

Even my most amicable friendship ended with heartbreak…

I had to gather myself, regroup, refocus, and let go.

"The Bounceback"

You can't handle me not wanting you or giving away your love
You don't like the fact that I could fit another like a glove
You can't take me moving on. You don't like knowing I'm taken
You can't stand to look at me and see the beast has reawakened
The confidence has returned and the sex drive is high
You hate that I am up and happy and unafraid to fly
You're mad that I can love again; that I can be hopeful and open
You're jealous that I am with someone who's honest and unbroken
Someone who loves me for all the flaws you claimed only you would tolerate
Someone who speaks positivity despite their own heartbreak

Someone who trusts me like you never could and
who I could trust the same
Someone who came and stayed consistent
without the lies and games
Someone with no agenda, whose ego wasn't
bruised
Someone who loved me for being me and not just
someone to use
Someone who knows what they really want
And doesn't have to hide
Someone who bares themselves to me and puts
their pride aside
Someone who lets go of the past and knows what
he can lose
Someone that doesn't need reminding about who
he should choose

"Giving In"

How will I ever get what I expect?
Always running, never looking back
Even with everything I've been through
I'm done with running so I give in to you

As we embrace I know I am ready
You hold me still and keep me steady
You pull me back when I pull away
You speak the words that I won't say

I've fought this feeling for far too long
I knew my feelings were far too strong
But I continued to suppress
Simply refusing to confess

My love for you was always there
But our fight was never fair
And I decided not to fight
I didn't know what Love was like

Now I'm ready to fight for you
Because I know what's right and true
I've never felt this complete
And it's never felt like this for me

Everything around me fades
I'm lost in you like you're a maze
I'm free falling into your space
And I can only see your face

You occupy my thoughts too much
I'm flooded every time we touch
It's never been this way before
It's time I say that I want more...

Once I allowed myself to feel all the pain, hate, regret, shame, and anger I was able to also feel the love. And once I learned to love myself again, I was able to shed my final tear with this letter…

Dear Narcissist,

You're such an empty soul

You only seek control

But I control myself

So you seek someone else

You hate you're insecure

You try to stay obscure

But I see all you hide

It's all about your pride

You're selfish and unsure

You'll never have much more

You take what you can get

Then you don't give a shit

You want me to react

You think I'll take you back

But I know far too much

So I just sit and hush

You're self-absorbed and vain

All you know is pain

And I know that you aim

To make us feel the same

You tell lies and deny

Deception's how you thrive

You're perfect in your cult

So you do not take fault

You keep up a facade

Your world is a mirage

But I can see it clearer

Dissolving smoke and mirrors

Deep inside you're shrinking

You want to see us sinking

You need the upper hand

But tall is how I stand

And my dear narcissist

I'm not here to assist

I will not feed your highs

You won't be my demise

You can't have my affection

This is your rejection

I will not be your puppet

I can not fill your bucket

It took so much courage for me to write this; and even more courage to publish it. But I am so glad I was able to. I've never dealt with so much uncertainty before. Even when I was making bad decisions I was always sure. Because of that, this project scared the shit out of me. But I faced my fears and bared my tears. Now I present to you my final encomium.

"Heaux Phase"

Yep, I was wildin out
Fucking niggas I aint even care about.
Being careless, living crazy
Really outchea making babies

I was moving around fast
Full throttle and it's all gas
But boy when shit got bad it was all bad
Living life wild, making people big mad

And I did the shit TWICE
Feeling people, but never spending nights
In and out like a burger joint
Friends asking "what's the fuckin point?!?"

But I was heartbroken
Brutally honest, so no lies were ever spoken
I was upfront, they knew we were just fuckin
Grown ass people, no time for thumb suckin

I needed something else to feel
So hoeing became my fucking thrill
And it kept my heart pumping
Beating out my chest with our bodies bumping

Judge me not... or do
If you gon call me names then call me True
I know, I know; I've done the most
And that's why I will make this toast

Toast to myself for doing me
Experiencing my shit and living free
Sometimes that's what it takes to be great
So this heaux phase is something I will celebrate.

Cheers!

www.ingramcontent.com/pod-product-compliance
Lightning Source LLC
LaVergne TN
LVHW051506070426
835507LV00022B/2950